NT
7/19

Pet Expert

HAMSTERS & GUINEA PIGS

By Gemma Barder

WAYLAND
www.waylandbooks.co.uk

PET EXPERT:
HAMSTERS & GUINEA PIGS!

Hamsters and guinea pigs make great pets. Fact. They are fun, energetic and love to play, but how much do you know about these furry mini-mammals?

In this book you'll find advice on which pet to choose, how to make the perfect home for them, and how to keep your pet happy and healthy. Plus there's some absolutely paw-some hamster and guinea pig facts to discover. How did guinea pigs become pets? What is the world's biggest hamster? Get reading to find out!

CONTENTS

LITTLE PET, BIG LOVE!

SCURRY THROUGH TIME

FURRY FRIENDS

Learn all about the most popular types of hamster and guinea pig. The little things that make them different will help you choose the best pet for you.

HAMSTERS vs GUINEA PIGS

■ A hamster cage won't take up as much room as a guinea pig run.

■ Guinea pigs are more social than hamsters.

■ Guinea pigs live longer than hamsters.

■ Some guinea pigs require lots of grooming.

AMERICAN GUINEA PIG

The American Guinea Pig is the most popular breed of guinea pig in the world. It has a calm, sweet nature and a soft, easy-to-manage coat, which makes it the perfect pet. It is happiest when spending time with other guinea pigs and its owner.

ABYSSINIAN GUINEA PIG

This stylish guinea pig is popular because of its fabulous hairstyle. Its fur grows in spiky swirls called rosettes and these create its distinct look. The Abyssinian needs to be groomed and it can be quite naughty, too!

2 years

8 years

Hamsters live for an average of two years while guinea pigs can live for an average of eight years.

CAMPBELL'S DWARF HAMSTER

These little fluff balls are about 10 cm long. Dwarf hamsters are sociable and are happy to share their cage with another hamster. They are silvery-grey in colour and can be a bit more nervous than Syrians, so they won't like to be handled as much.

SYRIAN HAMSTER

If you've ever looked for a hamster in a pet shop, you've probably spotted this little chap! Syrian hamsters are usually golden brown in colour and grow to around 15 cm long. Although they like spending time with their owners, they don't like sharing their cage with another hamster.

DID YOU KNOW?

When your guinea pig is happy they might jump about or do little hops. This is called popcorning!

RARE RODENTS

From wild islanders to those who need sun cream, hamsters and guinea pigs have been living alongside humans for a long time. Some need more care and attention from us than others.

THE SANTA CATARINA'S GUINEA PIG

This rare guinea pig comes from a tiny island in the state of Santa Catarina, Brazil. There are only 45–60 of them left in the world, making them an endangered species. The entire population of this special breed of wild guinea pig lives in a 4,000 m² space (about the size of an athletics track).

SKINNY PIGS

Skinny Pigs certainly don't look like your average guinea pig! They are born without hair and so they need to eat a bit more to keep their body temperature up. But in most other ways they are just like a regular guinea pig and have a calm, sociable personality.

DID YOU KNOW?

Skinny Pigs have similar skin to humans, so if you take them out in the sunshine they need to wear sun cream to stop their skin burning!

DWARF WINTER WHITE RUSSIAN HAMSTERS

Dwarf hamsters are a common species of pet hamster, but it is quite rare to find the pure white version. Although they may look white, most Dwarf Winter White Russian Hamsters will have grey patches on their noses and ears.

EUROPEAN HAMSTER

This wild species of hamster can grow up to 35 cm long and has distinct black fur on its tummy. The European Hamster has become endangered in some areas due to it being hunted for its fur, or because farmers see it as a pest. Luckily, environmentalists are working to protect the species.

DID YOU KNOW?

In 2017 the Flemish government pledged €800,000 to stop the Flemish (European) Hamster from becoming extinct in Flanders, Belgium.

PERSONALITY

With tiny paws and twitchy noses, hamsters and guinea pigs are the sweetest pets around. Read on to discover how these furry companions are different, but so similar, too!

HAMSTERS

Most prefer to be kept alone in their cages. Keeping some types of hamsters in pairs might mean they end up fighting!

Their little bodies are most energetic during the night and often keep their owners awake as they scurry around their cage.

Hamsters are very quiet when they squeak. In fact, some of their noises are ultrasonic, which means they can only be heard by other hamsters!

SHHH ...

GUINEA PIGS

They sleep on and off all through the day and night, so are neither completely noctural nor diurnal.

HELLO THERE!

These clever pets can make around 11 unique sounds. When they get to know their owners, they will start to 'chatter' to them.

Aww, little guinea pigs can get lonely, so it is recommended that they are kept in pairs (or more if you have the space).

TRAITS THEY SHARE

NIBBLE
They love gnawing and nibbling on anything from cardboard to the sides of their cages.

STROKE
Guinea pigs and hamsters like to be stroked, but hamsters might get fidgety and want to be put down.

RUN
They are both really active and love to run around, play with toys and stretch their little legs.

PUPS

There are lots of differences between hamster and guinea pig pups, but there is one thing they definitely share – cuteness!

HAMSTER PUPS

Hamsters are born blind, deaf and completely furless, although it doesn't take them long to develop. After two weeks they have fur and start to open their eyes. Hamster pups need to stay with their mothers until they are a month old – before that they should not be handled by humans.

Hamster babies soon start to look like miniature versions of their parents!

GUINEA PIG PUPS

Unlike hamsters, guinea pigs are born fully alert and with fur. In fact, they are just like tiny versions of full-grown guinea pigs! The other big difference is that guinea pig pups can be handled almost straight away, so they get used to being around people very quickly.

Guinea pig pups don't waste any time. They want to begin exploring!

FACT FILE

■ Guinea pigs have between two and four pups in a litter.

■ They can eat solid food straight away, and grass after a few weeks.

■ A pup weighs around 100 g (the same as a bar of soap).

■ Most guinea pigs are about one month old when they are taken to a new home.

1 pup

20 pups

Litters of hamsters can have anywhere between one and 20 pups!

LITTLE PET, BIG LOVE!

Although guinea pigs and hamsters are very easy-going pets, these intelligent little characters still need lots of love and attention to keep them happy.

DINNER TIME

Guinea pigs should have a diet rich in vitamin C and fibre. They eat a combination of hay, grass, special pellet food, fresh leaves and herbs. And like all pets, they need a supply of fresh water.

Hamsters should be given dry food containing the vitamins and minerals they need, as well as fresh fruit and vegetables, such as carrots, bananas and sweetcorn!

KEEPING CLEAN

Guinea pigs like to keep clean and they will do most of their cleaning themselves. They need to be brushed regularly (twice a day for long-haired breeds) and their nails should be trimmed once a month.

Hamsters don't usually need to be washed or brushed, but if they do get messy you can use cotton wool balls and a little warm water to wipe away any dirt.

DID YOU KNOW?

Not all lettuce is good for guinea pigs. Iceberg lettuce can give them bad stomach pains and cause kidney problems. Romaine lettuce is the best.

FUN TIMES

Hamsters love to be entertained, so take them out of their cage at least once a day. Some hamsters like balls and wheels, but exploring (and hiding) are their favourite. Try making a fun hamster run using cardboard tubes.

Always keep an eye on your hamster when they are playing outside their cage!

Guinea pigs love to be social, which is why they should be kept with at least one other guinea pig – or even two or three! They also love to play and explore, so make sure you give them lots of attention and freedom within a safe, secure area.

RODENT RULES

Can guinea pigs go in hamster wheels? Can hamsters eat too much? Avoid common mistakes by following these simple hints and tips.

HAMSTERS – DO:

get the right size wheel for your hamster. If the wheel is too big or too small, it could injure its back.

scoop your hamster from underneath when picking it up. If you grab them from above, they might confuse you for a predator.

keep your eyes on your hamster when they are roaming free. They are small and can disappear very easily!

GUINEA PIGS – DO:

keep them indoors when it is cold or very hot. Guinea pigs are sensitive to heat and can overheat as well as get too cold.

research the right type of bedding to use in your cage (turn over the page to find out more).

interact with your pet each day. Even if you don't have time to sit and play, make sure you say hello and give them some attention.

HAMSTERS – DON'T:

❌ wake your hamster up to play when they are sleeping. Hamsters are nocturnal and like to sleep lots during the day.

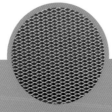

❌ use a wheel made out of mesh as this will damage their feet.

❌ let your hamster overeat. Hamsters can get overweight and this causes health problems.

GUINEA PIGS – DON'T:

❌ put a guinea pig in a hamster ball. Unlike hamsters, they have rigid backs that could get damaged inside a ball.

❌ use cedar or pine wood chippings for bedding as it can be toxic to small animals.

❌ keep guinea pigs in the same cage as other animals, such as rabbits or ferrets. They won't get along and the guinea pig could get hurt.

✔ FOOD FOR GUINEA PIGS & HAMSTERS ❌

 carrots   cucumber

 broccoli   kale

 cauliflower   tomatoes

 tomato leaves and stalks   potatoes

 meat   almonds

 chocolate   biscuits

THE COSIEST CAGE

From choosing the right bedding to finding the perfect toys, creating an interesting and snuggly home for your furry little friend will keep them happy and healthy.

HAMSTER HOME

Your hamster's cage will need to be at least 80 cm by 50 cm and made of plastic, metal or glass. If you choose a cage with metal bars, make sure they are close together to stop your hamster from escaping. Safely close the cage door after you have put your hamster back inside.

BLISSFUL BEDDING

The floor of your cage should have a thick layer of special hamster bedding. Never use sawdust or wood shavings as these could hurt your pet. You'll also need to put some nesting material in their hidey house – shredded toilet tissue works really well for this.

HOUSEWORK!

Bedding that has been soiled will need to be cleaned out each day and all bedding should be replaced once a week. Each month you should remove all bedding and furniture and give your cage a good clean.

GUINEA PIG DIGS

The more guinea pigs you have, the more space they will need. For two guinea pigs your cage or pen will need to be at least 150 cm by 70 cm. It's up to you whether you have a pen or a cage, but it will need the following things!

BEDTIME!

Guinea pig bedding can be made of paper or straw, or special guinea pig bedding material. You can make your bedding extra soft by adding fleece blankets to the bottom of your cage before you start to add the bedding material.

GUINEA GIGGLES

Guinea pigs like to be entertained, but they also like to have lots of dark places to snuggle up and hide. Willow bridges, large tunnels and soft, squidgey hidey houses are perfect for playful pigs.

FOOD AND DRINK

Guinea pigs need to eat fresh fruit and vegetables, hay and pellets that contain lots of vitamins and minerals. They'll also need a water bottle filled with fresh water fixed to their cage or pen.

DID YOU KNOW?

You can use a bowl to feed both hamsters and guinea pigs or scatter their food around the cage – or a combination of both!

SCURRY THROUGH TIME

Discover how guinea pigs were given as special gifts and the unusual history of the hamster!

ALL BUT GONE

By the 1920s, hamsters had been hunted so much that they were virtually extinct and only a few remained.

1700-1800

1920s

1930s

HAMSTER HISTORY

Here, there, everywhere! As you might have guessed, the Syrian Hamster originated in Syria. At one time, there were so many hamsters in the wild that farmers hunted them as pests and sold their fur.

AN AMAZING DISCOVERY

An archaeologist working in Syria discovered a female hamster and 12 babies. He then transported them back home and bred them as pets to be exported around the world.

A FRIEND AND GIFT

In 1000 BCE, guinea pigs were often given as gifts on birthdays and even as wedding presents.

2000 BCE   **1000 BCE**   **CE 1700s**

GUINEA PIG PROGRESS

Guinea pigs have been kept as pets for over 4,000 years! They are native to South America and were kept for food and as pets for children in Peru and Bolivia.

ON THE MOVE

When traders from Europe came to South America, they took guinea pigs back with them and they became popular pets across the world.

RENOWNED RODENTS

From Hollywood films to the White House – hamsters and guinea pigs are just too cute not to be famous!

HAMSTER HEROES

RHINO

In 2008, the world was introduced to *Bolt*, the film about a TV dog who thought he had superpowers. Rhino the hamster is Bolt's biggest fan and although he spends most of his time in an exercise ball, Rhino became so popular that Disney made a short, spin-off film all about him!

FOOTBALL SUPERSTAR

Hammy the Hamster is the mascot of Scottish football team Hamilton Academical F.C. The team was founded in 1874, and Hammy was given a makeover in 2017 to give him a cheeky, cheerful look. Fans of Hamilton Accies love watching Hammy warm up the crowd before each home game.

GUINEA PIG STARS

PRESIDENTIAL PIGS

Theodore Roosevelt (1858–1919) was the 26th president of the USA, and also a big fan of guinea pigs! His pets became the most famous guinea pigs in the 1900s and had strange names like Admiral Dewey, Dr Johnson, Bob Evans, Bishop Doan and Father O'Grady.

DID YOU KNOW?

A famous painting, which hangs in the UK's National Portrait Gallery, shows an Elizabethan girl holding a typical brown and white guinea pig. Queen Elizabeth I (1533–1603) had a pet guinea pig.

NORMAN

The Secret Life of Pets told the story of two apartment dogs as they struggled to get along in New York, but it also introduced us to lots of other city dwelling pets – including Norman, a happy, positive guinea pig who's always up for adventure!

RODENT HEROES

Hamster pensioners and speedy guinea pigs. Take a look at the world's most remarkable rodents.

58 species

3 species

There are 58 species of rodent on the critically endangered list, and three of these are possibly extinct.

QUICK AS A FLASH!

A guinea pig called Flash, (like this one), was recorded as taking just 8.81 seconds to run 10 m in 2009, making him truly the Usain Bolt of all rodents!

HAMSTER'S GIANT COUSIN!

A capybara is sometimes described as the world's biggest hamster, but it's actually not a hamster at all. It is the world's biggest rodent, though, and can grow up to 64 cm tall and over one metre long!

ПОЧТА СССР

3^к

1985

Пятипалый карликовый тушканчик

This stamp was used in the former Soviet Union over 30 years ago to celebrate the Jerboa.

DID YOU KNOW?

The oldest living hamster lived for seven years (a hamsters' usual life span is two years).

TEENY TINY RELATIONS

The Baluchistan Pygmy Jerboa is the smallest rodent on Earth (and also possibly the cutest!). It weighs less than 30 g and measures only four centimetres tall. It stands on its hind legs, which makes it look like a tiny kangaroo rather than a rodent.

ALL ABOUT RODENTS

- There are over 2,000 species of rodents in the world.
- These include everything from squirrels to porcupines.
- Rodents' teeth never stop growing, which is why they like to nibble and gnaw.
- They don't like the smell of peppermint. Some people plant it to keep rodents away.

THE LONG-ISH JUMP

Truffles is the holder of the record for the longest jump by a guinea pig. He managed to leap over a gap measuring 48 cm, which is quite a challenge for a pet with such little legs!

0 cm   48 cm

DID YOU KNOW?

The oldest living guinea pig lived for 15 years. Their average lifespan is between seven and nine years.

FURRY FACTS

Want to know even more about your favourite rodent pair? Read on to discover more fabulous facts!

1 VERY CHEEKY!

Hamsters store food in their cheeks to save it for later on. The food can make their bulging cheeks double in size!

2 TAKE A CLOSER LOOK

Guinea pigs have four toes on their front paws and only three on their back paws.

3 TWILIGHT'S NOT JUST FOR VAMPIRES

Hamsters are crepuscular, which means they are most awake during twilight hours.

4 WHAT'S IN A NAME?

Guinea pigs are not pigs, or from the country Guinea in Africa. It is believed they picked up the piggy name because of the high-pitched squeaks they make.

5 CLEVER QUEUE

When guinea pigs walk together they always do so in single file with the largest guinea pig at the front and the young in the middle.

YOUR FAVOURITE FURRY FRIEND

Can we match your personality to your dream pet?
Answer the questions and follow the flow to find out!

Cute!

Relaxing

DO YOU PREFER BEING WITH FRIENDS OR RELAXING ON YOUR OWN?

WHAT'S BETTER: SMALL AND CUTE OR FURRY AND FRIENDLY?

Friendly!

Afternoon

Being with friends

ARE YOU A MORNING PERSON OR AN AFTERNOON PERSON?

Morning

Not sure

Maybe

DOES YOUR HOUSE HAVE PLENTY OF ROOM?

WOULD YOU LIKE MORE THAN ONE TYPE OF PET?

Yes, lots!

Yes!

ARE YOU ACE AT MAKING MAZES?

Totally!

I'm OK

I'd rather not

HAMSTER

You'd like a pet that isn't too much trouble, but that you can enjoy playing with and caring for. You don't mind if they like to sleep a lot, you'll give them all the love they need, right when they want it.

WOULD YOU MIND BRUSHING YOUR PET?

I'd love to

Sometimes

No

GUINEA PIG

Just like you, guinea pigs like to be social and active! Even if you've never had a pet before, you can't wait to be the best pet owner around and want to make sure you do things properly.

HAVE YOU HAD A PET BEFORE?

Yes

A bit

IS CLEANING OUT CAGES BORING?

I don't mind

BOTH!

You love animals and might even have a pet already. You love the idea of having lots of pets to take care of, but make sure you know how much care and attention each furry friend needs.

QUIZ!

It's time to test everything you have learned in your book! Are you the pet expert on hamsters and guinea pigs?

1 WHAT IS IT CALLED WHEN GUINEA PIGS DO LITTLE JUMPS AND FLIPS?

a) pop dancing
b) pop hopping
c) popcorning

2 WHAT IS THE NAME OF THE SPECIAL HAIRLESS BREED OF GUINEA PIG?

a) Skinny Pig
b) Bald Pig
c) Furless Pig

3 WHY CAN'T SYRIAN HAMSTERS BE KEPT IN PAIRS?

a) they could spread diseases
b) they might fight
c) they stop eating

4 WHICH RODENTS ARE BORN BLIND?

a) hamsters
b) guinea pigs
c) both

5 WHICH RODENTS WOULD LOVE A WHEEL IN THEIR CAGE?

a) hamsters
b) guinea pigs
c) both

The answers can be found on page 30.

6 WHY SHOULDN'T YOU KEEP GUINEA PIGS WITH OTHER SPECIES OF PET?

a) they might get hurt
b) they steal all the other pets' food
c) they'll hide all the time

9 WHAT WAS THE NAME OF THE HAMSTER IN THE DISNEY FILM, *BOLT*?

a) Rhino
b) Hippo
c) Wolf

7 HOW OFTEN SHOULD YOU GIVE YOUR HAMSTER CAGE A THOROUGH CLEAN OUT?

a) once a year
b) once a week
c) once a month

10 WHAT IS THE LARGEST RODENT IN THE WORLD CALLED?

a) hare
b) capybara
c) porcupine

8 WHICH ENGLISH QUEEN HAD A GUINEA PIG AS A PET?

a) Queen Mary
b) Queen Elizabeth I
c) Queen Victoria

GLOSSARY

BEDDING
The material used to line your pet's home and make a bed out of.

BREED
A group of animals with similar characteristics and appearance

CAGE
A container for your pet to live in, closed on all sides. It can be made of metal, plastic, wood or glass.

COAT
The type of fur your pet has. It could be long, short, rough or silky.

DIET
What an animal eats

DIURNAL
Active during the day rather than at night

EXTINCT
For a breed or species to no longer exist in the world

FLEMISH
The main language of northern Belgium

GNAWING
Biting and nibbling persistently

GROOMED / GROOMING
To brush, clip and clean your pet

HIDEY HOUSE
An enclosed, dark area for your pet to snuggle up in

LITTER
A collection of baby animals born at the same time to the same mother

NOCTURNAL
Active at night rather than during the day

POPCORNING
The excited jumps and hops a guinea pig does when they are happy

PREDATOR
An animal that wants to kill or eat another animal

PUPS
Baby hamsters and guinea pigs

RODENT
The name given to the group of animals including hamsters, guinea pigs, rats, mice and many more

SOILED
To have been weed or pooed on by your pet

SPECIES
A group of animals that are capable of sharing genes and interbreeding

ULTRASONIC
Sound that is higher than the level a human can hear

QUIZ ANSWERS

1. C,   2. A,   3. B,   4. A   5. A,   6. A,   7. C,   8. B,   9. A,   10. B.

INDEX

First published in Great Britain in 2019 by Wayland
Copyright © Hodder and Stoughton, 2019
All rights reserved
Editor: Dynamo Limited
Designer: Dynamo Limited
HB ISBN: 978 1 5263 0863 4
PB ISBN: 978 1 5263 0864 1

Printed and bound in China
Wayland, an imprint of
Hachette Children's Group
Part of Hodder and Stoughton
Carmelite House
50 Victoria Embankment
London EC4Y 0DZ
An Hachette UK Company
www.hachette.co.uk
www.hachettechildrens.co.uk

The website addresses (URLs) included in this book were valid at the time
of going to press. However, it is possible that contents or addresses may
have changed since the publication of this book. No responsibility for any
such changes can be accepted by either the author or the Publisher.

Picture acknowledgements:

All images courtesy of Getty Images iStock apart from:
© Film Company Disney/AF Archive/Alamy: 20cl.
Lynne Cameron/PA Archive/PAi: 20b.
ImageBroker/Alamy: 3tr, 7tr, 29bl.
Eric Isselee/Shutterstock: front cover r, 1r.
Sonja Jordan/Alamy: 7c, 28br.
Igor Kovalchuk /Shutterstock: front cover l, 1l.
DmitryPron/Shutterstock: 14cr.
Tierfotoagentur /Alamy: 5br.
© Universal Pictures/Entertainment Pictures/Alamy: 21c.

(Key: cl-centre left, cr-centre right, c-centre b-bottom, bl-bottom left,
br-bottom right, r-right, l-left)

Every attempt has been made to clear copyright. Should there be any
inadvertent omission please apply to the publisher for rectification.